ARMED SERVICES

Jim Brush

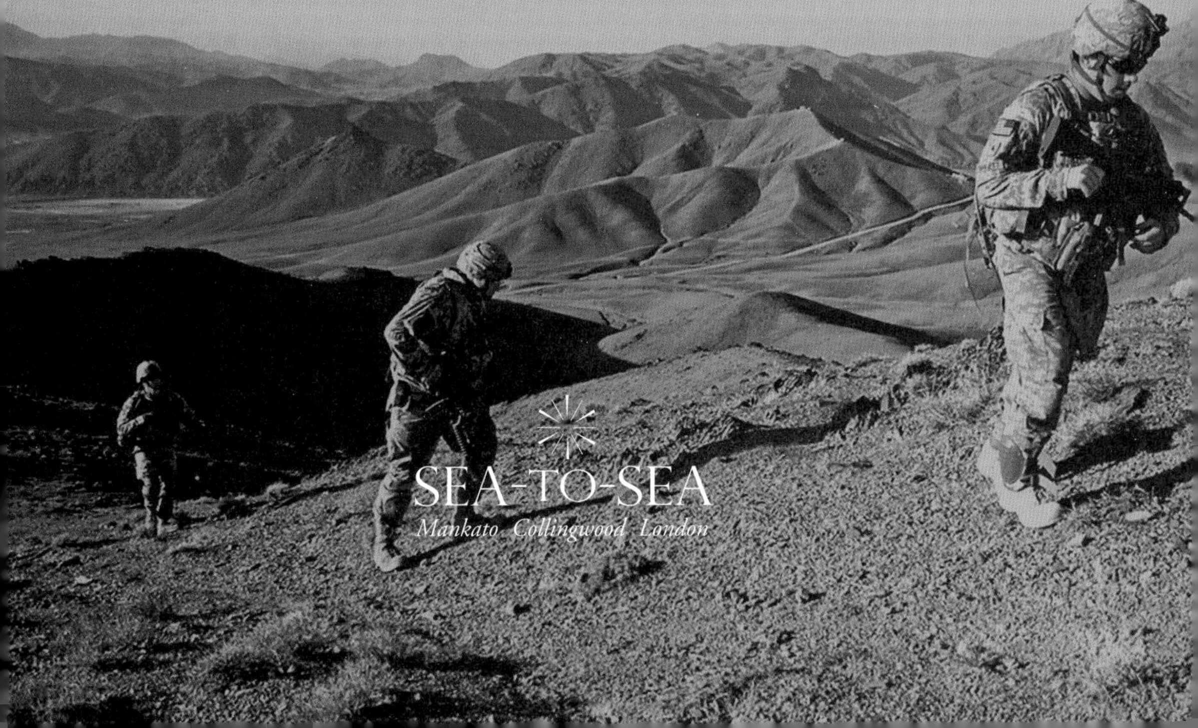

SEA-TO-SEA
Mankato Collingwood London

This edition first published in 2012 by
Sea-to-Sea Publications
Distributed by Black Rabbit Books
P.O. Box 3263, Mankato, Minnesota 56002

9 8 7 6 5 4 3 2

Published by arrangement with the Watts Publishing Group Ltd, London.

A CIP catalog record for this book is available from the Library of Congress.

ISBN: 978-1-59771-291-0

Series editor: Adrian Cole
Art director: Jonathan Hair
Design: Simon Borrough
Picture research: Luped

Acknowledgments:
AFP/Getty Images: 27br. Gregory Bergman/Alamy: 29. Ben Birchall/PA Archive/Press Association Images: 13.
Commonwealth of Australia 2009: 12. Cpl Ian Forsyth RLC/Crown Copyright/MOD: 16. Steve Gibson/
istockphoto: 11cl. Lhfgraphics/Dreamstime.com: 19t. Peter McDiarmid/Getty Images: 14b. John Moore/Getty
Images: 28t. Olivier Morin/AFP/Getty Images: 5b. naphtalina.com/istockphoto: 5t.
Christian Phillipe Paris/epa/Corbis: 7bl. Reuters/Corbis: 22. Jeremy Richards/Shutterstock: 7cr.
Royal Navy/Crown Copyright: 23cl, 23r. WO2 Fiona Stapley/Crown Copyright/MOD: 18.
Graham Taylor/Shutterstock: 27t. UN Photo/Logan Abassi: 9, 10. UN Photo/Marco Dormino: 19b.
UN Photo/Evan Schneider: 17c. U.S. Air Force/Senior Airman Christopher Bush: 25t.
U.S. Air Force/Master Sgt Jack Braden: 25b. U.S. Air Force/Master Sgt. Andy Dunaway: 26. Photo Courtesy
of U.S. Army/Staff Sgt. Russell Bassett: 7tr.   Photo Courtesy of U.S. Army/Sgt. Jason Dangel: 28b.
Photo Courtesy of U.S. Army/SSG Adam Mancini: 1, 4, 20t. Photo Courtesy of U.S. Army/Capt. James Reid,
Combined Task Force Castle: 17b. Photo Courtesy of U.S. Army/Spc. Monica Smith, 3rd CAB, 3rd ID Public
Affairs: 21b. Photo Courtesy of U.S. Army/Phil Sussman: 20b. Photo Courtesy of U.S. Army/Spc. Richard Del
Vecchio: 6t. Photo Courtesy of U.S. Army/Werbefotografie: 14c. Photo Courtesy of U.S. Army/Capt. Richard
Ybarra: 21t. Photo Courtesy of U.S. Navy/Mass Communication Specialist 2nd Class Erik Barker: 11br.
Photo Courtesy of U.S. Navy/Mate 2nd Class Ryan Child: 15. Photo Courtesy of U.S. Navy/Mass
Communication Specialist 2nd Class David Didier: 7br. Photo Courtesy of U.S. Navy/Mass Communication
Specialist 2nd Class Greg Johnson: 8. Photo Courtesy of U.S. Navy/Photographer's Mate 1st Class Brian
McFadden: 27bl. Philip Wallick/Corbis: 24. en.wikipedia.org/wiki/File: USAF_roundel_1947: 7tl.

*Every attempt has been made to clear copyright. Should there be any inadvertent omission please
apply to the publisher for rectification.*

February 2011
RD/6000006415/001

Contents

Fighting Forces

The armed services are the military forces of a country or nation. Highly skilled and well-trained men and women defend their country using machines such as tanks, ships, and aircraft.

These U.S. soldiers from 4th Infantry Regiment are on patrol in Afghanistan.

The armed services operate on land, at sea, and in the air, and can be sent anywhere around the world. They fight in wars, but they can also keep the peace in other countries by stopping rival groups from attacking one another.

ACTION STATS

China has the largest armed services in the world, with more than 2.25 million troops. The U.S. Army has the most equipment, with over 7,500 tanks and more than 3,500 aircraft.

Fighter aircraft are an important part of any armed service.

In the past, armies relied on having millions of soldiers to win battles. Today, most armed services are much smaller, but the troops are more highly trained and better equipped. The Swedish Navy, for example, uses modern technical systems on its stealth ship, HMS *Helsingborg*, that allow it to share information easily with the Swedish Army and Air Force.

HMS Helsingborg *is a Visby-class corvette. Its unusual shape makes it hard for enemies to detect it using radar.*

The Three Services

Most countries have three armed services—the army, navy, and air force. Some nations also have a separate coastguard or military police force.

In the past, the army fought on land, the navy went to sea in ships, and the air force flew aircraft. Today, the three armed services work together and are more of a mix. Many armies have their own helicopter units to move soldiers quickly. Marines are ground troops who use navy boats to attack from the sea.

AF FACTS

The U.S. 101st Airborne is one of the most famous divisions in the world. They take part in air assaults (above). The division is nicknamed the "Screaming Eagles."

How can you tell the services apart? Each country has a different style of uniform, and each service has its own insignia and uniform design.

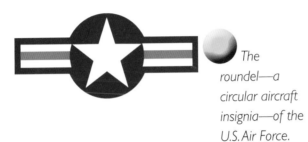

The roundel—a circular aircraft insignia—of the U.S. Air Force.

Ground units, such as those in the army or marines, wear uniforms to match the surroundings. For example, they are green or brown, to blend in with forests. This makes it more difficult for the enemy to see them.

Air force pilots, such as this French fighter pilot, wear special gear when in the air.

log book

inflatable collar (for use if a plane crashes at sea)

insignia

flight suit

helmet

visor

boots

A special uniform, known as dress uniform, is worn for important occasions. These Indian soldiers are wearing dress uniform on parade.

Navy uniforms are usually blue, like the color of the sea.

7

What Do They Do?

The main job of the armed services is to defend their country and its people. Men and women put their lives on the line so that people can live in freedom.

AF FACTS

Radar is an electronic system that tracks the position and speed of aircraft, ships, and vehicles. It is an important part of a country's defense, because it can warn of possible attacks.

Air traffic controllers check the radar that scans an area more than 435 miles (700 km) wide.

If your country was invaded, the armed services would try to defend you. They also help to protect you from terrorists and criminal gangs. Not all troops fight though. Many work behind the scenes in support roles, such as technicians or mechanics. In 2008, $1.3 trillion was spent on the armed services worldwide.

Many countries send their soldiers to help the United Nations keep peace around the world. Sending forces to a troubled region can stop a small conflict from turning into a large war in which more people could die.

"Peace is a full-time job. The UN has over 100,000 Peacekeepers on the ground, in places others can't or won't go, doing things others can't or won't do."

Actor George Clooney

Brazilian UN troops unload supplies in Haiti.

Different Roles

Today, the armed services of many countries have different roles to play. These can include aid missions in natural disaster zones—when people are left homeless and without food after a hurricane or earthquake. They also swing into action when people need to be rescued.

 These Brazilian UN peacekeepers are on duty in Haiti during a food riot after a hurricane hit the island.

When there is a hurricane or earthquake, the armed services come to the rescue. Their helicopters, boats, and vehicles go to work even when the roads have been destroyed. They bring emergency food and shelter for the victims of a disaster.

In many countries, such as Canada, the U.S., Denmark, Brazil, and the UK, the navy and air force have search and rescue services. They rescue stranded or injured hikers or climbers around the coasts and mountains.

"Experience gained in the harsh conditions of Afghanistan has helped injured patients in the UK."
Lt. Col. Jeremy Henning

This search and rescue Westland Sea King helicopter is part of the Australian Navy.

AF FACTS

In 2007, four Royal Marines in Afghanistan strapped themselves to the sides of two Apache helicopters in a daring attempted rescue mission. Apache helicopters have no room for passengers.

An injured man is winched up into a helicopter from a boat in the Caribbean.

Where In the World?

The job of the armed services takes them across the globe. Some countries have large bases, known as garrisons, in other countries where their help is needed.

 These Australian troops are part of an international force on duty in East Timor.

Countries such as the United States, France, and the UK have lands overseas they want to protect. They may also have an agreement with another country to help protect them. For example, Denmark currently has a naval base in Greenland.

Other countries send military forces overseas to keep the peace or patrol the seas. In 2006, Australian troops were sent to East Timor to stop riots and a rebellion by local soldiers.

"In the Navy you can request to serve in a variety of locations. I know many sailors who lived in Italy, Britain, Hawaii, Spain, or Japan."
Theodore Scott, U.S. Navy

This British "Jackal" crew are on patrol in Helmand, Afghanistan.

ACTION STATS

In 2008, U.S. armed forces had 1.4 million personnel on active duty, though the total number of U.S. troops is 2.3 million. The U.S. operates 865 bases and facilities abroad. Total U.S. military spending in 2008 was greater than $600 billion.

Daily Life

Life for people in the armed services is very different to a regular job—they can be called into action at any moment.

Fitness training in a gym is just part of daily exercise for people in the armed services.

The men and women in the armed services obey orders and follow strict rules. This helps them stay focused when they are under pressure in a battle.

These recruits are drill training as part of their basic training.

AF FACTS

Basic training includes:
- **Skill-at-arms (learning to use a rifle)**
- **Shooting**
- **Fieldcraft (how to work on patrol)**
- **Physical training**
- **Adventure training (such as climbing)**

ACTION STATS

Servicemen and women spend long periods away from home on a mission, or "tour of duty." This can last a few months or several years.

Fitness training is a big part of military life. Soldiers spend hours in the gym and on assault courses (below). They must be able to carry heavy equipment—weighing around 130 pounds (60 kg)—and run for several miles.

Working Together

Whatever the challenge, members of the armed services rely on the friendship and support of their team. They must work together to achieve their goals—whatever they may be.

Life in the armed services is all about teamwork. Fighter pilots, tank crews, and ship's gunners all rely on other people around them to do their job. While on duty they train, eat, and sleep with these same people.

The crew of this Challenger 2 battle tank is made up of four members: the commander, gunner, loader/operator, and driver.

DS 79 AA

The army, navy, and air force also work together as a team. Ships can launch aircraft and provide a base for soldiers to launch an attack from. Aircraft also support ships or soldiers on the ground.

"You make strong friendships that last a lifetime."
Soldier in the Australian Army

Australian and U.S. engineers work together to rebuild a bridge.

Soldiers from Pakistan help unload supplies.

The Army

The army operates on the ground. It is organized into different units that have specific skills. Officers are the leaders who give the orders, while soldiers do jobs such as driving a tank or operating a radio.

A member of the International Security Assistance Force (ISAF) in Afghanistan checks a 117F satellite radio.

AF FACTS

Signals **corps provide communications and IT—everything from the radios carried by a platoon, to large satellite dishes linking command centers on different continents.**

Every army unit is led by an officer. Stars, stripes, and "pips" on a uniform show his or her rank. The higher an officer's rank, the more troops he or she commands. Those shown below are from the U.S. Army.

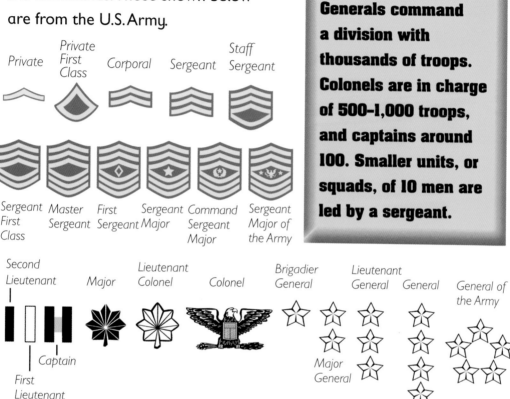

Private   Private First Class   Corporal   Sergeant   Staff Sergeant

Sergeant First Class   Master Sergeant   First Sergeant   Sergeant Major   Command Sergeant Major   Sergeant Major of the Army

Second Lieutenant   First Lieutenant   Captain   Major   Lieutenant Colonel   Colonel   Brigadier General   Major General   Lieutenant General   General   General of the Army

A Sri Lankan medic examines a woman's eye. Medical teams don't just treat injured soldiers, they also assist during aid operations.

Within an army, different units, or corps, do a particular job. The infantry and tank corps fight the enemy on the ground. Engineers build bridges and keep the equipment running. The logistics corps organize the weapon and food supplies, while medical corps treat the wounded.

Army Equipment

The army uses many types of equipment. Troops carry weapons for fighting. Vehicles carry them into battle. Soldiers also need radios, mine detectors, and other equipment.

AF FACTS

The Javelin missile system (left) can be used against tanks, buildings, and even helicopters. It has "fire and forget" technology, which means that it locks onto a target even if the launcher moves.

The infantry (soldiers on the ground) carry weapons such as rifles and machine guns. Large guns, called artillery, fire explosive shells a long way. Tanks also carry powerful guns. Their tracks allow them to drive across deserts or muddy fields. Other armored vehicles carry the infantry into action.

U.S. soldiers of the 17th Field Artillery Regiment fire an M198 155 mm howitzer.

The infantry use a wide range of nonlethal technology, too. Radios and systems such as Land Warrior help troops keep in touch, and metal detectors help troops clear mines hidden in the ground. Field kitchens and hospitals support troops on the move.

This infantryman is wearing the Land Warrior system, which includes a computer and radio link to the whole patrol.

ACTION STATS

Chinooks, such as this one, can quickly drop off and pick up troops.

The Chinook is used by different armed services around the world. A versatile, twin-engine, twin-rotor helicopter with a top speed of 195 mph (315 km/h), its wide loading ramp at the rear is used primarily to move troops and heavy equipment.

The Navy

The navy operates at sea using ships and aircraft. As well as defending a country from attack, it patrols the seas and supports the army.

A navy is particularly important to nations with long coastlines, such as the United States, Canada, UK, and China. It guards the surrounding seas and keeps trade routes open. As well as its fighting and peacekeeping duties, a navy patrols fishing grounds and oilfields.

Ships have an important part to play in the defense of many countries.

AF FACTS

Every navy has a history. The modern French Navy, under Napoleon III (1808–73), helped to build the French Empire. Napoleon used new technologies, including steam and ship armor.

There are different ranks in the navy. Admirals may command a whole fleet, while ships are commanded by a captain. Ordinary sailors are known as "able seamen."

The Captain stands with other naval officers above the ship's bridge.

"A lot of people do get seasick when we first sail but after a couple of days it's just a few who still get sick."
Nursing Officer Grundy, Royal Australian Navy

"Battle stations" is the highest level of alert a ship can be on. These radar operators are wearing fireproof clothing, known as antiflash gear.

The Air Force

The air force operates in the skies. Planes and helicopters are used to fight enemy aircraft, as well as bomb the enemy. They also support troops on the ground.

Lockheed Martin/ Boeing's Raptor in flight.

ACTION STATS

The U.S.-built F22 Raptor has stealth technology and is one of the best all-round fighter planes in the world. The U.S. Air Force currently flies 139 Raptors, which have a top flying speed of 1,500 mph (2,410 km/h)!

The air force also keeps the peace by flying over troublespots. Its planes and helicopters deliver supplies and carry out search and rescue missions. In an emergency, they can be used to evacuate (move) people from a danger zone.

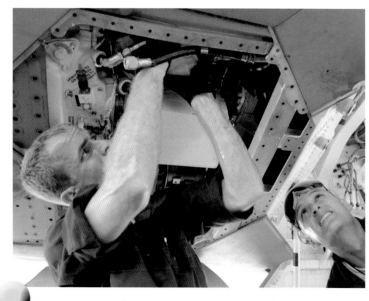

Planes are organized into units known as squadrons. The pilots who fly the planes rely on a team of engineers, mechanics, and other ground crew to keep their planes running.

Two airmen conduct important engineering checks.

"I joined because I wanted to became a pilot. It was my dream ever since I was a little kid." PFC (Private 1st Class) Charles Landeros, who works on Blackhawk helicopters in the U.S. Army.

Pilots are briefed before every mission. There is a lot of information to take in, such as the timing, the target, and the tactics.

Pilots in a briefing room prepare for a training exercise. Training instructors will also fly during this exercise to test new students.

Military Aircraft

An air force has fast combat aircraft to attack targets in the air and on the ground. Larger, slower planes and helicopters are used to move troops and equipment.

The A10 Thunderbolt is nicknamed the "Warthog."

AF FACTS

A10 Thunderbolt II—targets tanks and other armored vehicles
- Guns: 1x30 mm GAU-8/A Avenger cannon, 1,174 rounds
- Rockets: Hydra 70, CRV7 70 mm and Zuni rockets
- Missiles: 2xAIM-9 Sidewinder and 8xAGM-65 Maverick
- Bombs: many combinations

Fighter planes are used in air-to-air combat. Bombers and helicopters are used to attack targets on the ground. These aircraft use advanced systems to help them find their way, or navigate. Weapons include cannons (machine guns) and missiles suited to attacks on planes, tanks, ships, and buildings.

ACTION STATS

AH64 Apache Longbow— helicopter gunship (below)
- Guns: 1 30x113 mm M230 cannon, 1,200 rounds
- Rockets: Hydra 70 FFAR rockets
- Missiles: combination of AGM-114 Hellfire, AIM-92 Stinger, and AIM-9 Sidewinder

AF FACTS

Eurofighter Typhoon— multirole fighter (above)
- Guns: 1x27 mm Mauser cannon
- Missiles: AIM-9 Sidewinder, AIM-132 ASRAAM, and IRIS-T
- Bombs: laser-guided

Helicopters can also be used to attack forces on the ground and to deliver troops and supplies. One of the deadliest helicopters is the AH64 Apache Longbow. It is in service with five different air forces: the U.S., UK, Israel, Japan, and the Netherlands.

An Apache taking off (below), and a close-up view of its rocket and missile systems (right).

Changing World

The challenges faced by the armed services are always changing. Today, there are new threats from terrorists and countries that have developed nuclear weapons.

In the military, a lot of work goes into planning for the future. Some countries have created a rapid reaction force that is always ready for action. This is made up of all three services—army, navy, and air force. It also includes special forces troops.

In the future, new technology may start to play an even more important role. There are already UAVs (Unmanned Aerial Vehicles) that can be remotely controlled to take photos of enemy targets or even to attack them.

AF FACTS

Special forces are highly trained troops who often work behind enemy lines. The men above are using night-vision goggles, which allow them to see in the dark.

A UAV operator launches an RQ-7B Shadow 200. It will take up-to-date images of the surrounding area.

ACTION STATS

Countries such as Russia and the U.S. are trying to cut down their store of weapons of mass destruction. Both sides are hoping to reduce their nuclear weapons to 1,500 warheads each.

Many countries believe that the best way to keep the peace is to join forces with organizations such as the United Nations and NATO. By working closely with other nations, they hope to avoid conflict.

The USS Oriskany was taken out of service in 2006. The former aircraft carrier was sunk off the Florida coast to form a reef for sealife.

Fast Facts

- The U.S. Department of Defense requested $533.7 billion base budget for the year 2010. Some countries, including Iceland, Costa Rica, and Morocco, have no army.

- The armed forces of the UK, India, and Canada still have cavalry regiments—soldiers who do guard duties on horseback. However, they fight in tanks or other types of armored vehicles.

- The United States has the world's largest air force, with more than 6,000 planes and over 300,000 men and women on active duty.

- A Tristar fuel-tanker refuels other planes while they are still flying. It carries more than 22,450 gallons (85,000 liters) of fuel. That's enough to enable an average car to drive around the world three times.

- A navy often has a floating hospital so that members of the armed services can get the best medical care close to where they are fighting.

Glossary and Web Sites

Engineers—armed service that looks after all the equipment, builds bridges, and makes maps.

NATO—a military organization. Members include the U.S., UK, Canada, France, and Germany.

Natural disaster—events, such as a tsunami or earthquake.

Peacekeepers—military forces used to keep the peace, often by keeping two enemy forces apart.

Platoon—small group of soldiers.

Radar—device that tracks planes and ships using radio waves.

Signals—communications such as radios, which allow the armed forces to share information.

Stealth technology—smooth design invisible enemy radar.

Weapons of mass destruction—weapons that cause massive damage and loss of life, such as nuclear bombs.

www.navy.mil
Web site of the U.S. Navy, with hundreds of photos of ships and crews at work.

www.un.org/Depts/dpko/dpko
Part of the United Nations web site focusing on peacekeeping operations. It includes information about current operations, photos, and webcasts.

www.history.army.mil
Web site of the U.S. Army Center of Military History. It includes photos of past conflicts and has a searchable poster gallery.

Please note: every effort has been made by the Publishers to ensure that these web sites contain no inappropriate or offensive material. However, because of the nature of the Internet, it is impossible to guarantee that the contents of these sites will not be altered. We strongly advise that Internet access is supervised by a responsible adult.

Index